AROHA JOY

My Love Language

Copyright © 2020 by Aroha Joy

All rights reserved. No part of this publication may be reproduced, stored or transmitted in any form or by any means, electronic, mechanical, photocopying, recording, scanning, or otherwise without written permission from the publisher. It is illegal to copy this book, post it to a website, or distribute it by any other means without permission.

First edition

This book was professionally typeset on Reedsy.
Find out more at reedsy.com

This book is dedicated to God Almighty

Contents

Preface	ii
Acknowledgments	v
1 The Beginning of It All	1
2 What Is Love?	5
3 The Language of Words	9
4 Acts of Service: Love in Action	13
5 Quality Time: The Space Between Us	18
6 Acts of Service: A Silent Promise	23
7 Receiving Love	28
8 The Challenge of Vulnerability	32
9 Building a Future Together	37
10 The Promise of Tomorrow	41

Preface

I had always believed that love was something simple, a feeling that came easily when the right person entered your life. I never imagined that understanding love would require so much patience, effort, and communication. I first met Sam in a crowded café, a chance encounter that sparked something deep inside me. I felt a connection instantly, but I didn't realize then that it would lead me on a journey of self-discovery and emotional growth.

I learned early on that love wasn't just about grand gestures or intense passion; it was about understanding each other's needs and expressing affection in ways that truly resonated. I struggled at first to understand Sam's love language, especially when his actions didn't always align with my expectations. I expected constant words of affirmation, but I soon discovered that his love was shown through acts of service, something I didn't fully appreciate until I began to pay attention to the little things he did for me.

I found myself questioning whether we were truly compatible at times, unsure if our differences in expressing love could lead to long-term happiness. I was caught up in the notion that love had to look a certain way—one that mirrored my own desires and needs. I couldn't see the depth of Sam's love because I wasn't looking for it in the right places. I had to learn how to open myself up, to communicate my needs without placing unrealistic expectations on him.

I realized that in order for Sam and I to build a lasting relationship, I had to shift my perspective. I had to learn how to speak his love language and be more patient with myself in the process. I had to embrace the idea that love wasn't a one-size-fits-all concept. I began to appreciate Sam's quiet support and the ways he showed his love without words, finding fulfillment in the small acts that often went unnoticed.

I began to share my own vulnerabilities with Sam, slowly opening up about the fears and insecurities I had carried for years. I found that as I became more open, our bond grew stronger. I learned that my love language—words of affirmation—was just as important as Sam's, and that sharing it with him didn't make me weak, but human. I began to trust that he could meet my needs, and in turn, I learned to meet his.

I faced moments of doubt, questioning whether our differences in love languages would eventually drive us apart. I feared that if we didn't find common ground, we might lose each other. But I also realized that it wasn't about forcing each other into a mold, but about compromising and making space for both of our needs to be met. I discovered that love was a journey, one that required effort from both sides, but that the rewards were worth it.

I found myself growing more and more connected to Sam as we navigated the complexities of our relationship. We learned to communicate openly, to express our needs without fear of rejection. I learned that true intimacy came from vulnerability, and that the more we shared, the deeper our love became. I began to see our relationship not as a destination, but as an ongoing process of growth and discovery.

I realized that the key to a lasting love wasn't just about learning each other's love languages—it was about embracing change and growth. I had to let go of the notion that love was static, that once you found the right person, everything would fall into place. I learned that love was dynamic, evolving with every shared experience, every challenge, and every triumph.

I knew that the journey ahead would not always be easy. We would face challenges, moments of misunderstanding, and times when it felt like we were drifting apart. But I also knew that we had built a strong foundation, one that was rooted in trust, communication, and mutual respect. I realized that love, at its core, was about showing up for each other, day after day, and making the choice to continue loving despite the obstacles.

I looked ahead, knowing that whatever the future held, I was ready to face it with Sam by my side. I had learned the value of patience, of speaking my love language and listening to his. I had learned that love wasn't just about what you say or do, but about the intention behind it. I knew now that love was not a destination to be reached, but a journey to be experienced—together.

Acknowledgments

Thank you for your love and support

1

The Beginning of It All

Love had always been a complicated concept for me. Growing up in a small town where everyone knew everyone's business, love seemed more like an expectation than an experience. It was the kind of love that you saw on billboards, in movies, or in the occasional couple holding hands in the park. But it never felt real. It was always something that happened to other people, not me. At least, that's what I thought—until I met Sam.

I remember the first time I saw him like it was yesterday. It was a hot Saturday afternoon in late spring, and I was browsing through the new books at the local bookstore. The smell of freshly printed pages mixed with the faint aroma of coffee from the cafe corner. I was lost in my world, flipping through the pages of a romance novel, when I heard his voice.

"Excuse me," Sam said, his voice soft but confident. "Do you know if the new fantasy series by Alicia Thompson is in stock?"

I looked up, startled, to find a tall, dark-haired man with a gentle smile standing in front of me. His green eyes seemed to have an intensity that drew me in, yet there was a warmth that instantly made me feel at ease. I was struck by how he didn't seem like anyone I had ever met before. Not the type to blend in with the crowd, but still comfortable in his own skin.

"I think it's over there," I said, pointing to a section of the store. "Are you a fan of fantasy?"

He nodded, following my gaze toward the shelf. "Yeah, I've been reading a lot of fantasy lately. It's the escape I need after a long week at work."

I chuckled, recognizing that feeling all too well. "I get that. It's like you can leave your world behind for a while and dive into something completely different."

Sam smiled, and for the first time, I felt a strange connection—one I hadn't felt before. I couldn't place it, but there was something in the way he looked at me that made me feel seen. After a few more moments of casual conversation, he asked for my number.

"I'm Sam, by the way," he said, offering his phone. "I'd love to continue chatting, if you're up for it."

Something in my gut told me this was not just any other fleeting encounter. And for the first time in a long while, I said yes.

—-

Our first few months together were everything I had imagined love would be. We spent long hours talking about books, our favorite childhood memories, and the music that shaped our lives. He was thoughtful and funny, and the more time we spent together, the more I realized how much I wanted to be near him. We were connected in a way I couldn't quite explain, but I thought I was finally getting the hang of this whole "relationship" thing. I was in love, or so I thought.

But as time passed, I started to feel like something was missing. I couldn't put my finger on it, but it felt like I was speaking a language he didn't understand.

He was sweet, attentive, and kind, but I wasn't entirely sure if he truly "got" me. Every time he would do something nice for me—like bring me coffee or help me with a task—I felt grateful, but there was a nagging feeling in the back of my mind that said, *Is this really what I need?*

And then, there were the moments when he would sit next to me, hold my hand, and we'd talk. His words were always comforting, but they never seemed to reach the place inside me that longed for something deeper. I loved spending time with him, but I wanted more than just a companion. I needed a connection that would reach beyond the surface, something that resonated on a level I couldn't quite explain.

I began to feel frustrated. Why didn't he understand the importance of certain things? Why was it so hard for him to show his affection in ways that felt meaningful to me? I started to ask myself whether love was supposed to feel this complicated.

—-

One evening, after a particularly frustrating conversation, Sam and I found ourselves sitting on a park bench near the lake. The sun was setting, casting an orange glow across the water. He turned to me, his expression serious.

"Is something wrong?" he asked, his voice hesitant.

I hesitated, unsure of how to articulate what I was feeling. "I don't know, Sam. I just... I feel like we're not on the same page. I love spending time with you, but sometimes it feels like we're speaking different languages."

He furrowed his brow. "Different languages?"

I nodded. "Yeah. Like... you're giving me what you think I need, but it's not what I really want. I don't know how to explain it, but I think we might be missing something."

Sam looked down at his hands, processing my words. After a few moments of silence, he spoke again. "Maybe we just need to understand each other better. Figure out what we really need from one another."

I smiled softly. "Maybe."

—-

It was in that moment that I realized I needed to learn more about love, not just in the romantic sense, but in a way that helped me understand my own needs and how to communicate them. As the days went by, I began to explore what it meant to love someone and to be loved in return. I discovered that love isn't just about grand gestures or sweet words; it's about the small, everyday things that make you feel seen and heard.

And so, my journey into love languages began. Little did I know, this journey would lead me to a deeper understanding of myself, Sam, and what it truly meant to love—and be loved—in return.

2

What Is Love?

The question of love had always intrigued me. Growing up, I was fed on the idea of grand gestures, the kind you see in fairy tales—love at first sight, sweeping romance, and passionate declarations. My parents, though loving, were more practical than romantic. I never really saw them express affection openly, not in the way I imagined love should look. Sure, there were small gestures—my dad making my mom a cup of tea every morning or my mom packing him his favorite snacks for his long workdays—but it didn't feel like the kind of love I saw in movies or heard about from friends. It felt... steady.

When Sam and I first started dating, I thought I understood love, at least to some extent. But as I started to spend more time with him, I realized that the image I had of love was incomplete. It was like I had a blurry picture of a painting, and I was just now beginning to see the details. There were things I didn't know about myself, about Sam, and about what it meant to truly connect with another person.

Sam and I had been dating for six months when we had our first serious disagreement. It wasn't anything dramatic, but it was enough to make me pause. I had invited him over to my place for dinner. I had spent the entire day preparing a three-course meal, hoping to surprise him. When he arrived, he seemed distracted, barely noticing the effort I had put into the meal. We ate in silence, save for the occasional comment about the food.

Afterwards, I cleaned up while he sat on the couch, scrolling through his phone. That's when it hit me—he wasn't looking at me the way I expected. He wasn't noticing the small details, the ones I thought should matter. The conversation was dull, and I felt like we were worlds apart.

"I thought you'd like it," I said, trying to break the silence. "You didn't even say anything about the food."

He looked up, slightly surprised. "It was great. You're an amazing cook."

But it didn't feel like enough. I needed more than just a compliment. I wanted him to recognize the effort, the thought I had put into the evening. I needed him to appreciate the details, to know that the meal was my way of showing him I cared.

"I don't know, Sam. It just feels like you're not really *here* sometimes," I said, my voice betraying my frustration. "I put all this effort into planning the evening, and you barely noticed."

He blinked, his expression confused. "I didn't realize it meant that much to you. I'm sorry if I hurt you. I just thought we were hanging out, enjoying each other's company."

It was in that moment I realized something: we weren't on the same wavelength. My feelings of disappointment weren't about the dinner itself; they were about the connection I felt was missing. I wanted more than just physical presence—I wanted emotional engagement, a deeper connection that went beyond the surface level.

—-

In the days that followed, I couldn't stop thinking about the conversation. I replayed it over and over in my head, trying to understand why I was so upset. That's when it hit me: I had been expecting something that Sam didn't know how to give. My need for emotional depth, for the recognition of small, thoughtful gestures, had clashed with his approach to love. Sam was kind, he was present, and he was willing to help me when I needed it—but he didn't seem to understand my need for acknowledgment in the same way I did.

I realized that love wasn't a one-size-fits-all emotion, and I needed to learn more about myself—and about him—if I wanted our relationship to work. This realization led me down a rabbit hole of exploration. I started to read books, talk to friends, and search for answers. One book, in particular, stood out to me: *The Five Love Languages* by Dr. Gary Chapman.

As I read, everything clicked into place. The book described how people express and receive love in different ways. The five primary love languages—Words of Affirmation, Acts of Service, Receiving Gifts, Quality Time, and Physical Touch—seemed to describe everything I had been feeling, but hadn't yet been able to articulate. It was like I had stumbled upon a map that showed the way to understanding not only Sam but myself as well.

The chapter on *Words of Affirmation* was particularly eye-opening. I realized that I craved validation, praise, and heartfelt words of encouragement. It wasn't enough for Sam to simply be there physically or do things for me; I needed to hear that I mattered, that my efforts were seen and appreciated. I thought back to the dinner, and it was clear that his lack of verbal acknowledgment had left me feeling unseen.

—-

I began to examine my relationship with Sam through the lens of these love languages. I noticed how he expressed love differently than I did. While I sought emotional depth and validation through words, Sam expressed his affection through *Acts of Service*—like helping me move furniture, fixing things around the apartment, or making sure I was comfortable. He didn't always verbalize his feelings, but he showed his love through action. It was clear that he cared, but he didn't always express it in a way that spoke to me.

That realization didn't make me love him less—it made me understand him better. I realized that we had been speaking different love languages all along, and the key to making our relationship work wasn't just about figuring out what I needed, but also understanding how Sam needed to show love.

So, I began to explore my love language further, and with that, I started to understand Sam's as well. I needed to communicate my feelings more clearly and let him know what I needed from him. I also needed to be more open to the way he expressed his affection, without dismissing it just because it didn't look like mine.

—-

In those early days of self-discovery, I learned that love isn't just a feeling; it's a language, one that can be translated if both people are willing to listen. Sam and I had a long way to go, but I knew that understanding love languages was the key to building the kind of relationship we both wanted.

3

The Language of Words

After discovering the concept of love languages, I couldn't stop thinking about how they applied to my relationship with Sam. The idea that people express and receive love in different ways made so much sense to me. I had always felt a deep desire for verbal affirmations—those little words of encouragement, praise, and affirmation that make me feel seen and valued. Sam, on the other hand, didn't naturally speak that language, and I found myself questioning whether I was asking too much of him.

It was late one evening when I decided to talk to him about it. We had been having dinner together, and for the umpteenth time, I felt myself growing quiet as my mind wandered. The food was great, the setting was cozy, and Sam was his usual self—charming, caring, and completely unaware of the storm brewing inside me. I couldn't go on pretending that everything was fine. I needed to explain how I was feeling, even if it made me vulnerable.

"Sam, can we talk about something?" I asked, setting down my fork.

He looked up, pausing mid-chew, a concerned expression replacing his easygoing demeanor. "Of course. What's on your mind?"

I took a deep breath, gathering my thoughts. "I've been thinking about how we express love, and I don't think I've been clear about what I need from you. I... I need to hear it. I need to hear the words, Sam."

His brow furrowed slightly, and I could tell he was processing what I had just said. "You want me to say more? Like... I love you, or something?"

I nodded, relieved that he was listening. "It's not just about saying 'I love you,' though that helps. I mean the little things—the kind of words that make me feel like you see me, appreciate me. When you do something nice for me, I need you to tell me that you see the effort I put in. Or even just to acknowledge how much I care about you. I need those words to feel secure in our relationship."

Sam was silent for a moment, seemingly lost in thought. He shifted in his seat, running a hand through his hair. "I don't really do that. I mean, I show you I care by doing things for you, like fixing stuff around your apartment or cooking dinner. But I never really thought about how important it is to say those things out loud."

I felt a pang of disappointment, but I didn't want to make him feel bad. He was trying, even if it wasn't in the way I had imagined. "It's just how I understand love. I need the reassurance, the words. It's not about the actions being less meaningful, but words are what make me feel loved and connected."

"I get it," he said slowly, leaning forward. "I guess I've always believed that actions speak louder than words. I thought that if I showed you I care through what I do, that would be enough. But if words matter to you, I'll try to do better."

His willingness to understand and meet me halfway brought a sense of relief. I wasn't sure how this would work in the long run, but at least we were talking about it, which was a start.

—-

Over the next few weeks, I began to notice small changes in how Sam communicated with me. He still expressed his love in the ways he always had—helping me with tasks and surprising me with sweet gestures—but he started to be more intentional with his words. One evening, while we were curled up on the couch watching a movie, he turned to me and said, "You know, I really appreciate how patient you are with me. I'm learning a lot from you."

It wasn't a grand romantic declaration, but to me, it was everything. It was simple, but it was heartfelt, and it made me feel seen. I smiled and squeezed his hand, grateful for the effort he was putting in.

A few days later, I tried something new myself. I had always been good at expressing my feelings through words, but I realized that I had also neglected to show my appreciation for Sam in his preferred language—Acts of Service. He had always been a man of action, and while I had taken it for granted, I decided to make more of an effort to show him that I saw the things he did for me.

I baked him his favorite cookies and left a note on the kitchen counter that simply read, *Thank you for always being there for me. I love how you take care of me in so many ways*. I knew that he would understand this gesture, even if I didn't verbally say everything I was feeling.

When Sam saw the cookies, his eyes lit up. He smiled widely, pulling me into a hug. "You didn't have to do this," he said, clearly moved. "But it means so much to me. You're amazing."

It was in that moment that I realized love wasn't about doing everything perfectly; it was about making an effort to understand each other's needs and meeting them with an open heart. We didn't have to speak the same language to be in love—we just needed to learn how to communicate in a way that made each of us feel appreciated and cherished.

Over time, our relationship grew stronger as we both worked on understanding our love languages. Sam became more attuned to my need for verbal affirmations, while I learned to recognize and appreciate his expressions of love through actions. We no longer felt like we were speaking past each other. Instead, we were speaking to each other in the ways that mattered most.

Still, there were moments of frustration. Sometimes, Sam would forget to express his feelings verbally, or I would fail to recognize the ways he showed his love. But what mattered was that we were willing to try, to be vulnerable, and to listen to each other. The language of love was never meant to be perfect, but it was ours. And that was enough.

I learned that love wasn't just about how we spoke to each other—it was about how we listened, how we adapted, and how we were willing to meet each other halfway. In the end, that's what truly made the connection between Sam and me so special.

4

Acts of Service: Love in Action

The more I learned about love languages, the more I realized how little I truly understood about the different ways people express their affection. After discussing my need for words of affirmation with Sam, I began to consider his perspective. I saw the things he did for me every day—the way he fixed things around my apartment without being asked, the way he would pick up groceries for me on his way over, or how he would drive me home after a late meeting, even though it was out of his way. Sam's love language was clear: Acts of Service.

I knew that Sam wasn't the type to shower me with flowery words, but his actions spoke volumes. I began to appreciate those actions in a way I hadn't before. I had been so caught up in my own needs for verbal affirmations that I hadn't recognized how much he expressed his love through what he did rather than what he said.

One Saturday morning, I woke up to find Sam already in the kitchen, making breakfast. The smell of freshly brewed coffee and sizzling bacon filled the apartment, and the sound of pots and pans clattering brought a smile to my face. I wandered into the kitchen, half asleep, and leaned against the doorframe.

"Morning," I said, still rubbing my eyes.

Sam looked up and smiled. "Good morning. I thought I'd surprise you with your favorite breakfast. I figured you'd need the energy for all the errands we've got today."

I smiled back, feeling a warm rush of gratitude. "That's so thoughtful of you," I said, meaning it. As much as I loved breakfast, it wasn't just about the food—it was about the fact that Sam had taken the time to make it for me. It was his way of showing that he cared, of making my day a little easier, and I appreciated it more than words could express.

He handed me a plate piled high with pancakes, scrambled eggs, and bacon, and I could see how proud he was of his work. He had this way of taking pride in even the smallest tasks, and I loved that about him. As we sat down to eat together, I realized how much his love language impacted our relationship. It wasn't just about the big gestures; it was the little, everyday things that made a difference.

—-

Over the next few weeks, I began paying closer attention to the ways Sam showed his love through acts of service. There was the time he helped me assemble furniture after I had bought a new bookshelf, the way he offered to clean up after dinner without being asked, and even how he'd grab my coat from the back of the chair whenever we were heading out. I started to feel guilty. I realized I had been so focused on wanting words of affirmation that I hadn't been reciprocating his acts of love in a meaningful way.

One afternoon, as we sat on the couch, I decided to bring it up. "Sam, I've been thinking a lot about everything you do for me. And I don't think I've been very good at showing you that I appreciate it. I'm used to getting my love from words, but I see now that you show love through actions. I want to do more to show you how much that means to me."

Sam's eyes softened, and he placed his hand over mine. "I never expected you to do anything in return. I do it because I care about you, and it makes me happy to help. But if it means something to you, I'd love to see what you come up with."

That was all the encouragement I needed. I began to think about how I could show Sam my appreciation for his acts of service. While words were my preferred way of expressing love, I knew that I needed to step outside my comfort zone and learn to express my affection through actions, just as he did.

—-

A few days later, Sam came over to my apartment after work, tired from a long day. He slouched onto the couch, rubbing his eyes. I could tell he was exhausted, and something inside me shifted. I didn't want to just sit there and wait for him to do everything. I wanted to take care of him, just as he had taken care of me so many times before.

I stood up and walked to the kitchen, deciding to make him a cup of tea, something warm to help him unwind. While the kettle heated up, I grabbed his favorite mug and placed a lemon wedge on the counter, just the way he liked it. When the water was ready, I poured it into the cup and set it in front of him, offering a smile.

"Here you go," I said, sitting beside him. "I know you're tired. Thought you could use something to help you relax."

He looked at me, surprised, but then a small smile spread across his face. "You really didn't have to do this," he said, his voice warm with appreciation.

"I know," I said, "but I wanted to. You always take care of me, and I want to show you that I care too."

He took the cup in his hands, savoring the warmth. "You know, I think I've been a little spoiled by you," he said with a chuckle. "But this is really nice. Thank you."

That simple act—making him tea—was more meaningful than I had expected. I felt a sense of fulfillment in knowing that I had given him something that mattered, even if it was small. It wasn't just about the tea; it was about showing him that I recognized the effort he put into our relationship, and I was willing to do the same for him.

—-

Over the next few weeks, I continued to find small ways to express my love through actions. I picked up his favorite snacks from the store when he was working late, made him dinner after a long day, and even took care of his laundry when I noticed his hamper was overflowing. Each time, I saw a little more light in his eyes, a little more warmth in his smile. It was a reminder that love wasn't just about speaking the right words—it was about showing up for each other, even in the quiet, everyday moments.

One evening, Sam and I were sitting on the balcony, enjoying a glass of wine as the sun set. He turned to me, his expression serious but soft. "I've been thinking about everything you've been doing for me lately," he said, his voice full of emotion. "I know I don't always express myself the way you do, but I see how much you're trying. And I just want you to know that it means the world to me. You're incredible."

I felt a warmth spread through my chest. I knew Sam wasn't the type to always verbalize his feelings, but hearing him say that, in his own way, made my heart swell with happiness. I had found my way to speak his love language, and it had made all the difference.

In that moment, I realized something profound. Love wasn't just about finding someone who understood you perfectly—it was about being willing to meet each other where you were. Sam and I came from different places, with different needs and different ways of expressing affection. But in learning to speak each other's love languages, we had found a deeper, more fulfilling connection.

Acts of service had become our silent promise to one another: I will show up for you, not just when it's easy, but when it's hard, when we're tired, or when we're feeling unappreciated. Because love isn't just a feeling—it's a choice. And every day, we chose each other.

5

Quality Time: The Space Between Us

It was a typical Saturday afternoon, and the sun was shining brightly through the windows of the living room. Yet, despite the beauty of the day, I felt a strange sense of unease. Sam and I had been spending time together over the past few months, but there was something missing. We had fun, we laughed, and we even communicated well most of the time, but I couldn't shake the feeling that we were drifting. We were physically present, but emotionally distant.

It wasn't that I didn't care for Sam—I did, deeply—but I realized that in our busy lives, we had become accustomed to spending time together without truly being present. There were too many distractions, too many things to do, and often, we would sit next to each other on the couch, scrolling through our phones, watching TV without really engaging with one another.

I decided it was time for a change. I had learned about the importance of quality time as a love language, and it was clear that Sam and I needed to invest more in each other—not just in passing moments, but in meaningful connection. It wasn't about spending more time together; it was about how we spent that time.

I sent Sam a quick message: *How about we make today about just us? No distractions. I'll make dinner, and we can just talk, no phones, no TV.*

He responded almost immediately: *Sounds great. I'll be home in an hour.*

—-

When Sam walked through the door that evening, I was in the kitchen, chopping vegetables for a homemade stir-fry. The scent of garlic and ginger filled the apartment, and I was determined to make this night special—not just with the food, but with the attention we gave each other.

"I'm starving," Sam said, walking over to the counter to give me a quick kiss on the cheek. He seemed to be in a lighter mood than usual, which made me feel good. I knew that what we were about to do wasn't going to be easy, but I was ready to take the plunge.

"Perfect timing," I said, flashing him a smile. "Dinner will be ready soon. Why don't you go sit down? We'll eat when it's done."

He raised an eyebrow. "Are you sure? You don't need help?"

I shook my head. "Nope. I've got this. I just want us to sit down together, no distractions."

Sam gave me a puzzled look but didn't say anything more. He nodded and headed to the living room. A few minutes later, I joined him, placing our plates of food on the coffee table.

We sat together, and for a while, there was nothing but the clinking of forks and the soft hum of background noise. I was starting to feel awkward. I had asked for this space, this time for us to focus on each other, but now that we were together, I wasn't sure where to begin. I knew I had to let go of the distractions, but that didn't make the silence any less uncomfortable.

Finally, Sam broke the silence.

"Is this what you meant by no distractions?" he asked with a playful smile. "Because I've got to admit, this is a bit weird for me. We've never really done something like this before."

I smiled back. "I know. But I've been thinking a lot about quality time lately. I want us to really connect. Not just be together physically, but to actually focus on each other. No screens, no distractions."

Sam took a bite of his food and nodded thoughtfully. "Yeah, I get it. I think I've been guilty of letting things slip too. It's easy to just fall into routines, but I want to make this work. I want us to be present."

His words made me feel relieved. I wasn't alone in this desire to improve our connection.

We spent the next hour talking—really talking. We talked about everything and nothing. We shared stories from our childhood, laughed at the silly things that had happened to us in high school, and discussed our hopes and dreams for the future. As the conversation flowed, I began to feel more at ease. This was what I had been missing—the chance to really connect with Sam, to hear him, to be heard by him.

It wasn't just about talking; it was about listening. Listening to what Sam had to say, without distractions, without interruptions, without my own thoughts intruding on his words. And for the first time in a long while, I realized that I had been taking him for granted. I had been so focused on my own needs that I hadn't given enough attention to his, to what he was saying and how he was feeling.

As we finished dinner and moved to the couch, Sam put his arm around me, and I rested my head on his shoulder. The quiet between us was no longer uncomfortable—it felt peaceful, fulfilling. I knew we weren't perfect, but in that moment, I felt like we were exactly where we needed to be.

—-

Over the next few weeks, we continued to prioritize quality time. Some evenings, we would take long walks together, talking about everything under the sun. Other nights, we would cook together and enjoy a quiet dinner at home, just the two of us. We made an effort to leave our phones in another room and focus solely on each other. It wasn't always easy; old habits die hard. But each time we did it, I felt our bond growing stronger.

One weekend, Sam suggested we go on a spontaneous road trip. We didn't have a destination in mind; we just drove, letting the open road guide us. The journey was full of laughter, quiet moments, and deep conversation. We didn't need grand gestures or expensive dates—we just needed to be in each other's company, enjoying the simplicity of being present.

That weekend trip changed something between us. It wasn't about the places we visited or the things we did—it was about how we chose to spend that time together. In those moments, there was no rush, no hurry. Just us, existing in the same space, without any distractions.

—-

By the time we returned home, I knew that quality time was not just a concept for me—it had become a core part of how I wanted to experience love. It was more than just being physically together; it was about creating moments where we could be emotionally and mentally present for each other. And it wasn't always easy, but the effort was always worth it.

As I sat beside Sam that evening, looking out at the city lights from our balcony, I realized that love wasn't just about the big declarations or the grand gestures—it was in the quiet moments, the small conversations, the shared experiences. And as long as we made the time for each other, I knew our love would continue to grow, stronger and deeper, with each passing day.

6

Acts of Service: A Silent Promise

The first time I truly understood the power of acts of service was a rainy Thursday evening. I had just finished a particularly exhausting day at work, my mind reeling from back-to-back meetings, emails, and never-ending deadlines. I barely had time for lunch, let alone a moment to breathe. All I wanted to do was crash on the couch, order takeout, and forget about the world for a few hours.

When I walked into the apartment, the first thing I noticed was the warm scent of something simmering in the kitchen. I furrowed my brow, my exhaustion suddenly giving way to curiosity. Sam, who had been in charge of dinner that evening, usually stuck to simple recipes. I wondered what he was making and whether he had gone out of his way to surprise me.

As I walked toward the kitchen, I found him standing over the stove, stirring a pot of stew. The soft light of the overhead fixture cast a warm glow over his face. He looked up as I entered, his smile warm and easy, but his eyes were filled with something deeper—something more meaningful than just a simple smile. He could see the fatigue on my face, and he didn't need to ask how my day had gone. He already knew.

"I thought you might be hungry," Sam said, his voice gentle. "I made your favorite—chicken stew. I even baked some bread to go with it."

I felt a lump form in my throat. The exhaustion that had once weighed me down now felt lighter. It wasn't just the meal that hit me—it was the gesture behind it. Sam had taken the time to cook a full meal after his own busy day, not because he had to, but because he wanted to make things easier for me. It wasn't just about the food; it was about the care he put into it, the love behind the action.

"You didn't have to," I said, still standing at the doorway of the kitchen, a little overwhelmed by the unexpected kindness.

"I know," he replied, his tone matter-of-fact. "But I wanted to. I've noticed how tired you've been lately, and I thought this might help. We all need a little help sometimes, right?"

I walked over to him and hugged him tightly, my face pressed against his chest. His actions had spoken louder than any words could. In that moment, I realized how important acts of service were in a relationship—especially when words failed or when life became too overwhelming. It wasn't just about doing things for each other; it was about showing love in tangible, meaningful ways.

—-

As the evening unfolded, I found myself reflecting on the power of service. It wasn't just a grand gesture that made an impact; it was the small things. Sam didn't wait for me to ask for help or complain about how difficult my day had been. He anticipated my needs without hesitation, and in doing so, he had given me a gift—peace, comfort, and a reminder that I wasn't alone.

The next day, I woke up feeling more energized than I had in weeks. My mind wasn't consumed by the weight of the world, and I had the clarity to realize that love wasn't just about receiving—it was about giving, too. I had been so focused on my own needs and struggles that I hadn't considered how I could make things easier for Sam, how I could show him love in a way that he truly appreciated.

I decided to make it my mission to show him that I, too, could express my love through acts of service. It didn't have to be anything big or grandiose—just thoughtful actions that demonstrated my care and appreciation.

—-

The following Saturday, I planned a surprise for Sam. I knew he had been working on a new project for his startup and had been staying up late, often skipping meals or grabbing something quick from the fridge. I wanted to help him find a little balance, so I decided to prepare a meal for him to take to work the following week, something that would fuel him during his long hours.

I spent the morning cooking and packing his lunch—homemade lasagna, a side salad with fresh ingredients, and a homemade smoothie to top it off. When I was done, I carefully arranged everything in containers, making sure it looked as good as it tasted. I even included a small note that read: *For your busy days. I love you.*

When Sam came home later that evening, I handed him the bag. His eyes lit up as he opened it and saw the meal I had prepared for him.

"You did all this?" he asked, clearly surprised.

"Yeah," I said, smiling. "I know you've been working a lot lately, so I thought I'd take care of you for a change."

Sam looked at me, his expression softening. "You're amazing, you know that?"

"It's just a small thing," I replied, though inside, I felt proud. Proud because I had done something for him without any expectation of recognition or reward. It was my way of telling him that I saw him, that I appreciated the effort he put into making my life easier, and that I wanted to return the favor.

—-

As the weeks passed, acts of service became a cornerstone of our relationship. We didn't need grand gestures to show each other that we cared; it was the small, everyday actions that truly made a difference. Sam started waking up a little earlier to make me coffee before work, while I made sure he had a warm breakfast before heading out the door. He would clean up the kitchen after dinner without being asked, and I would take care of the laundry when I knew he had a busy week ahead. It wasn't about the tasks themselves—it was about the unspoken promise that we were there for each other, in both big and small ways.

One evening, Sam came home to find that I had organized his office for him. He had been complaining about the clutter for weeks, and though he hadn't asked for help, I knew it was stressing him out. When he saw the neat, organized space, he gave me a long hug, whispering, "Thank you," in my ear. It wasn't about the physical task of cleaning up his office—it was about me noticing his needs and offering my support.

—-

The more we practiced acts of service, the more our connection deepened. I realized that love, in its purest form, wasn't just about receiving affection—it was about giving, in ways that often went unnoticed, but always felt deeply significant. Whether it was preparing a meal, handling chores, or offering a simple gesture of support, these acts became our love language. They allowed us to show each other that we were not only partners but also teammates— always ready to support, love, and care for one another, no matter what life threw our way.

Through these small actions, I came to understand that love wasn't always loud—it could be quiet, subtle, and often, it was in the most unexpected places.

7

Receiving Love

For a long time, I thought love was only about giving. I was so focused on showing my affection, on finding ways to express how much I cared, that I never stopped to consider the equally important aspect of love: receiving it. It wasn't until I found myself in a vulnerable moment that I truly understood how difficult it could be to accept love from others.

It was a rainy Sunday afternoon when I first realized this. Sam and I had been together for over two years, and we had built a life full of shared moments—both big and small. We were comfortable together, our routines seamlessly blending. But that Sunday, something shifted.

I had been feeling out of sorts all week—overwhelmed with work, anxious about an upcoming project, and tired from the constant grind. I hadn't really given myself permission to rest, to stop and breathe, and it had started to catch up with me. I hadn't told Sam about how I was feeling, because I didn't want to burden him. After all, he had his own things to deal with. But that Sunday, my exhaustion hit me hard. I found myself curled up on the couch, unable to summon the energy to do anything—let alone pretend that I was fine.

Sam noticed almost immediately. He had been in the kitchen, preparing lunch, when he came into the living room and found me slouched on the couch, my face buried in a blanket. I hadn't even realized how much I had withdrawn until he sat down next to me, his presence suddenly enveloping me.

"You okay?" he asked, his voice gentle but concerned.

I hesitated, unsure of how to answer. I wasn't sure what was going on inside of me, and I didn't want to burden him with it. I was used to being the strong one, the one who handled everything without asking for help. But in that moment, I was tired. I didn't have the energy to pretend.

"I'm just... exhausted," I confessed, my voice barely above a whisper. "I don't know. I feel like I'm running on empty, and I don't know how to stop."

Sam didn't say anything for a moment. He simply reached for the blanket, pulling it up around me, and then, without a word, he went back to the kitchen. When he returned, he had a steaming mug of hot tea in his hands.

"I made your favorite," he said softly, handing it to me. "You don't have to do anything today. Just rest."

It was such a small thing. A cup of tea. A simple gesture. But it felt like so much more. Sam had seen that I needed help before I even realized it myself. He hadn't asked me to be strong, hadn't told me to push through it. He just let me be, offering me a moment of rest and care. For the first time, I allowed myself to fully surrender to the kindness he was offering, without feeling guilty, without thinking that I had to repay him immediately. I let myself receive.

—-

That afternoon, as I sat sipping my tea, I realized something crucial about love. I had always thought that showing love was a responsibility, an obligation.

I had prided myself on being someone who gave and gave, but I had never stopped to think about how it felt to be on the receiving end. It wasn't just about taking—it was about accepting love graciously, about trusting someone else with the parts of me that I usually kept hidden.

When Sam came back to sit next to me, he didn't try to fix things. He didn't give me a pep talk or tell me everything would be fine. Instead, he just stayed there, quietly. His presence alone was enough to make me feel supported, to make me realize that it was okay to lean on someone else. In that moment, I understood that love wasn't only about what I could do for others—it was also about allowing myself to be cared for, to be loved, and to accept that love without guilt or hesitation.

—-

Over the next few weeks, I found myself slowly embracing this new way of being. I started to open up more to Sam about how I was feeling, sharing the weight of my struggles instead of keeping them bottled up inside. He continued to support me, not by offering solutions, but by simply being there, offering a listening ear or a comforting gesture when I needed it most.

One evening, I came home from a particularly difficult day at work. I had received some disappointing news about a project I had been working on, and I felt defeated. When Sam saw my face, he didn't ask what was wrong immediately. Instead, he took my bag from my shoulder, guided me to the couch, and wrapped a blanket around me. It wasn't until I had settled in, with my head resting on his chest, that I found the words to explain how I was feeling.

"I'm just tired of not being good enough," I said, my voice cracking slightly. "I put so much into everything I do, and it never feels like it's enough."

Sam didn't respond with words. Instead, he held me tighter, his arms a silent reassurance. And in that silence, I realized that I had been trying so hard to do everything on my own, to prove my worth by constantly achieving. But in that moment, Sam showed me that love wasn't about doing—it was about being. It was about allowing yourself to be vulnerable, to be seen, and to trust that the people who truly love you will love you even when you're not at your best.

—-

As time went on, I became more comfortable with the idea of receiving love, not just from Sam, but from others as well. I realized that love wasn't a transaction—it wasn't something that needed to be earned. It was a gift, freely given, and all I had to do was accept it. I started to let go of the idea that I had to always be the one to fix everything, the one who carried the weight of the world on her shoulders. I allowed myself to lean on others, to trust that I didn't have to do it all alone.

And in doing so, I discovered a new kind of strength—the strength to be vulnerable, to accept love without shame or guilt. It was a quiet strength, one that didn't need to be loud or boastful. It was the strength of letting others in, of allowing myself to be cared for, and of trusting that I was worthy of receiving love just as much as I was capable of giving it.

8

The Challenge of Vulnerability

For as long as I could remember, I had built walls around myself—high, impenetrable walls. Walls meant to keep others out, to keep me from feeling too much, from being too exposed. Vulnerability was a concept I had never truly understood. It was something that made me uncomfortable, something that felt like a weakness. If I didn't allow myself to open up to others, then I wouldn't risk getting hurt. And that, to me, was the only way to stay safe.

But Sam had a different perspective on vulnerability. He believed that to truly love and be loved, one had to be vulnerable—one had to let go of the walls and expose the parts of oneself that were raw, unpolished, and real. He often told me that love could only flourish in the space created by openness and trust, and that the walls I had built were only keeping me from experiencing the depth of true connection.

At first, I was resistant to his ideas. How could I just let go of all the control? How could I allow myself to be so open, so exposed, when the world had shown me time and time again how easy it was to get hurt?

But as I spent more time with Sam, I began to realize that his approach wasn't about being reckless with emotions—it was about allowing space for vulnerability in a way that fostered intimacy and trust. Slowly, I began to see the cracks in my walls. I could feel myself inching closer to the truth that perhaps, just perhaps, I was capable of being vulnerable without it being a threat to my emotional well-being.

—-

One evening, after a long day, Sam and I were sitting on the couch, watching a movie. But I wasn't paying much attention to the screen. My thoughts kept drifting to the conversation we had had the previous week, the one about vulnerability. It had been a quiet conversation, one that took place as we sat on the balcony, overlooking the city lights. Sam had gently asked me why I held so much back from him, why I struggled to fully open up, even after everything we had been through together.

"I don't know," I had said at the time, my voice hesitant. "It's just hard for me to let people in. I've been hurt before. It's easier to keep things inside."

He had nodded, understanding but still patient. "I get it. But you don't have to carry everything alone. I'm here. And if you're willing to be vulnerable with me, to let me in, I promise I won't let you down."

At that moment, I had felt a surge of emotion, a mixture of longing and fear. I longed to let go, to be open and unguarded with him, but the fear of being vulnerable was stronger. I didn't want to be weak, I didn't want to be disappointed, and most of all, I didn't want to risk the one thing I held most dear—my independence.

But here we were, in our living room, the soft hum of the movie playing in the background, and I could feel that familiar sense of emotional distance between us. I wasn't allowing myself to truly connect with Sam. I was still holding back.

"Sam," I said, breaking the silence, "I've been thinking about what you said the other night."

He paused the movie and turned toward me, his expression soft but curious.

"I'm scared," I admitted, feeling the weight of my own vulnerability in those words. "I'm scared of being vulnerable. I'm scared of getting hurt. And I don't know how to let you in, even though I want to."

He took my hand gently in his, his touch warm and reassuring. "I understand," he said quietly. "But I want you to know that it's okay to feel scared. I'm not asking you to be perfect or to have all the answers. I'm asking you to trust me, to trust that I'm not going to hurt you. I'm here, and I want to be a part of your world in a real way. And that means seeing the parts of you that you think are too messy or too broken."

The sincerity in his voice made my heart ache. In that moment, I felt both terrified and relieved. Terrified of exposing my rawest self, but relieved that Sam was giving me permission to be human, to be imperfect, to be vulnerable.

—-

Over the next few days, I found myself reflecting on Sam's words more deeply. He had given me an invitation to trust, to share the things I had been holding back for years. But what would that look like? What would it feel like to let my walls down, to stop hiding parts of myself even from the person I loved most?

The more I thought about it, the more I realized that vulnerability didn't mean I had to lay bare every single detail of my life all at once. It didn't mean I had to expose myself in ways that felt too overwhelming. It meant taking small steps, one moment at a time, letting go of the need for control and perfection, and simply allowing myself to be seen.

—-

It wasn't long before I decided to take a small step. Sam and I were sitting in our favorite café, the warmth of the coffee cups in our hands matching the gentle warmth of the afternoon sun streaming through the windows. I looked at him and felt a sense of peace wash over me. This was the moment I had been waiting for. This was the moment I could let go.

"I've been thinking a lot about vulnerability," I said, my voice trembling slightly. "And I want to try. I want to start letting you in. But it's going to take time. I don't know how to do it all at once."

Sam smiled, his eyes filled with tenderness. "I don't need you to do it all at once," he said. "I just need you to be willing. I'll be here, no matter how long it takes."

His words, simple yet profound, gave me the courage to begin. It was okay to take my time. It was okay to feel afraid, as long as I didn't let the fear control me. Little by little, I allowed myself to open up more to him. I shared pieces of myself that I had kept hidden for so long—the insecurities, the old wounds, the things that made me feel vulnerable.

And with every word I shared, every layer I peeled away, I realized something important: vulnerability wasn't a weakness. It was an act of courage, of strength. It was the courage to trust someone enough to let them see the parts of you that you didn't want anyone else to see. And in that trust, love began to grow in ways I had never imagined.

—-

As I let myself be vulnerable, I found that the connection between Sam and I grew deeper. Our relationship became more intimate, more honest, and more real. For the first time, I felt like I was truly allowing someone to love me—not just the parts of me that were easy to love, but the parts that were messy and imperfect. And in return, Sam loved me even more for it.

Vulnerability wasn't a destination—it was a journey, one I was taking one step at a time. But with each step, I found more peace, more trust, and more love. And in the end, it wasn't the walls that had protected me all those years that had kept me safe—it was the love and vulnerability I was learning to embrace.

9

Building a Future Together

As time passed, something remarkable started to happen between Sam and me. What began as small acts of vulnerability, sharing pieces of ourselves we'd never shown anyone else, grew into a profound, almost unspoken understanding. We had opened the doors to each other's hearts, letting go of the fear that had once kept us distant, and in its place was a growing connection that I had never imagined possible.

It wasn't just about the big, grand gestures of love anymore. It was the small, everyday moments—those quiet, fleeting seconds of being present with each other—that had begun to define our relationship. It was Sam remembering to bring me my favorite coffee when I was feeling down or laughing at my corny jokes even when they weren't funny. It was me sending him random texts just to check in on his day, telling him how much I appreciated his kindness and support. It was in these small things that our love had begun to flourish, steadily and without force, like a plant growing in the quiet of the night.

But while our bond had deepened, we both knew that love wasn't just about enjoying the present—it was about creating something lasting, something we could build together. And that, in itself, was both exhilarating and intimidating. The future wasn't something either of us had fully addressed yet, but it lingered in the back of our minds.

One evening, as we sat together on the couch after dinner, the soft hum of the city outside, I found myself thinking about the next steps—what the future would look like for us. It felt like the right time to ask the question that had been on my mind for weeks.

"Sam," I said, my voice hesitant but determined. "What does the future look like for us? I know we're in a good place now, but... what happens next? I've been thinking a lot about it, and I think I'm ready to talk about it."

He turned to me, his eyes soft with understanding. Sam had always been the more grounded one, the one who could think through things logically while I often found myself lost in a swirl of emotions. He took a deep breath before responding, his tone calm but thoughtful.

"I've been thinking about it too," he said. "And honestly, I'm excited about what the future holds for us. I want to keep building this, keep growing together, and see where it takes us. I don't know what it looks like yet, but I know I want to do it with you."

The weight of his words hit me like a wave, but instead of feeling overwhelmed, I felt comforted. There was no pressure to have it all figured out, no rush to make decisions. It was the simplicity of knowing that we were both on the same page—that we both wanted the same thing. We weren't looking for perfection, just a shared commitment to each other.

Still, even with that assurance, there were parts of me that felt uncertain. My mind began to wander to the worries I had tried to push aside: Could we really build a future together? Would our differences cause problems in the long run? I had lived most of my life protecting myself from hurt, and the idea of fully giving myself to someone else—building a life with them—was terrifying. It felt like stepping off a cliff, not knowing whether there was solid ground below.

Sam must have sensed the change in my mood because he reached out and took my hand, squeezing it gently. "Hey, what's going on in that mind of yours?" he asked, his voice filled with concern. "You're quiet all of a sudden."

I exhaled slowly, gathering my thoughts. "I guess I'm just... scared. I've never really thought about the future in this way before. I've always kept my options open, kept my distance. But now, with you, it's different. I can see us building something together, but... what if I'm not ready? What if I can't give you everything you need?"

Sam's expression softened, and he leaned in closer, his eyes locking with mine. "You don't have to have all the answers right now. We're not in a race. We don't need to know everything. The only thing I need from you is your heart—just be here, with me, and we'll figure it out together. There's no pressure, no deadline. We have all the time we need."

His words, so simple and yet so profound, settled into my chest like a calming balm. It was okay to be unsure. It was okay to take things slowly. What mattered was that we were choosing each other every day, and that was enough. In that moment, I realized that the fear I had wasn't about whether we would be able to build a future—it was about letting go of control and trusting that everything would unfold in its own time.

We didn't need to have all the answers to the big questions. We didn't need to know every detail of what the future would look like. What mattered was that we were willing to face it together, hand in hand, open to whatever came next.

—-

Over the next few weeks, Sam and I continued to talk more about the future, sharing our hopes, dreams, and concerns. We discussed everything—from where we might live, to the kind of life we wanted to create, to the values we wanted to instill in our relationship. And though some of these conversations were difficult, filled with moments of doubt and uncertainty, there was also a sense of excitement that came with the unknown.

We didn't have a roadmap, but we had each other. And in that, we found comfort.

One Sunday afternoon, as we sat in the park, watching families and couples stroll by, Sam turned to me with a smile. "You know," he said, "I think we're doing it. We're building something together. Slowly but surely, it's coming together."

I smiled back, feeling a warmth spread through me. "Yeah, I think so too. It's a little messy, and we don't always know what we're doing, but I wouldn't want to do it with anyone else."

And in that moment, I realized that love wasn't just about the easy times, the moments of joy and laughter. It was about the work—the daily, sometimes difficult, work of building a life together. It was about being patient, being open, and trusting that, in the end, the pieces would fit together.

The future didn't have to be perfect. It just had to be ours. And with Sam by my side, I knew we could face whatever came next, together.

10

The Promise of Tomorrow

It had been nearly a year since Sam and I had opened up to each other about our fears and hopes for the future. In that time, we had grown more than I could have ever imagined. The connection we shared felt more profound than anything I had ever experienced. We had built a strong foundation—one made not just of love, but of trust, vulnerability, and understanding. And although there were still moments of doubt, I knew deep down that we were creating something real, something lasting.

But life, as it often does, had a way of throwing curveballs, testing even the strongest relationships. It was a Sunday afternoon when we faced one of the most significant tests of our relationship yet.

We had been discussing the next steps for a few weeks, and although we hadn't made any major decisions, the topic of moving in together had started to surface more frequently. Sam had just finished a big project at work, and I was preparing for an important presentation that could potentially change the direction of my career. It was a time of both excitement and stress for us, and while we were supportive of each other's ambitions, the weight of these pressures had begun to wear on both of us.

One particular afternoon, after a tense conversation about moving forward,

I could sense that something was off. Sam had been quieter than usual, his mind clearly preoccupied with something. I had been feeling the pressure of my own work and uncertainties about what was next for us, but Sam seemed distant, and I couldn't help but wonder if something had shifted.

"Hey, Sam," I said, as we sat in the living room, the evening light casting a warm glow through the windows. "Is everything okay? You've been acting kind of… distant lately."

He paused, looking at me with a mixture of hesitation and regret. "I've been thinking a lot, actually," he admitted. "About us. About moving in together. I know we've talked about it, but I'm not sure I'm ready for that step. It's not about you—I promise. It's just… I need more time to figure things out. To make sure we're both ready for that big change."

The words stung a little, though I knew they came from a place of care. Moving in together had always felt like the next natural step, but hearing him express doubt about it made my heart ache. I had imagined us taking that leap soon, and now, it felt as though everything we had been working toward was suddenly uncertain.

I took a deep breath, trying to collect my thoughts. "I get it," I said, my voice steady but soft. "I've been thinking about it a lot too, and I guess I just assumed that we were ready. But I don't want to pressure you. I want us both to be completely sure when we take that step. I guess I just want to make sure we're still on the same page."

Sam nodded, visibly relieved that I wasn't angry or upset. "I don't want you to think I'm pulling away from you. It's not that at all. I love you, and I want to spend my life with you. But I also want to make sure I'm bringing my best self to the relationship, and right now, I need to work on that. I need to be more present, more focused on us."

I looked at him, his eyes filled with sincerity, and I realized that, in his own way, he was trying to protect us. We had spent so much time building a strong foundation, and the last thing either of us wanted was to rush into something that could jeopardize everything we had worked for.

"I understand," I replied softly. "We don't need to rush. We've got time. The most important thing is that we continue growing together, no matter what."

The conversation left me with mixed feelings. On one hand, I was grateful for Sam's honesty, for his willingness to voice his concerns. On the other hand, I couldn't deny the ache in my chest—an ache that came from the fear of what the future might hold. Would we ever be ready for the next step? Would our love continue to grow at the pace we both needed?

That night, after a quiet dinner and some time to think, I found myself reflecting on everything Sam and I had shared. In those moments, I realized something important: love was never about perfection. It was never about having everything figured out or reaching certain milestones at the "right" time. Love was about showing up for each other, even when things were uncertain. It was about working together, side by side, and making a conscious effort to move forward—slowly, but steadily.

I was ready to take the next step with Sam, whenever that time came. But I also understood that the journey we were on was more important than the destination. The beauty of it was in the everyday moments, the way we supported each other, and the trust we had built.

In the days that followed, we continued to navigate our uncertainties with grace. Sam worked on his own personal growth, and I focused on my career, always reminding myself that we didn't need to have everything figured out. We just needed to be patient with each other and with ourselves.

A few weeks later, as we sat on the same couch where we had discussed our future, Sam turned to me with a smile that made my heart skip a beat. "I've been thinking a lot about what you said," he said. "And I want you to know that I'm ready to take the next step. Not because we have to, but because I want to, with you."

My heart swelled with joy, and I couldn't help but smile. "Are you sure?" I asked, my voice filled with hope and a little surprise.

Sam nodded, taking my hand in his. "Yeah. I'm sure. We've built something amazing, and I think we're ready to keep building, together. I'm all in, if you are."

And just like that, the weight that had been on my shoulders lifted. The uncertainty of the future no longer felt so heavy. I knew there would be more challenges ahead, more moments of doubt, but I also knew that we were ready to face them. We had already proven that we could build something real, something worth fighting for.

The promise of tomorrow was no longer a distant thought. It was something we were creating, together, one day at a time.

www.ingramcontent.com/pod-product-compliance
Lightning Source LLC
LaVergne TN
LVHW061604070526
838199LV00077B/7162